HOME OFFICE RESEARCH STUDY NO. 116

Keeping in Touch: Police–Victim Communication in Two Areas

by Tim Newburn and Susan Merry

A HOME OFFICE
RESEARCH AND PLANNING UNIT
REPORT

LONDON: HMSO

ISBN 0 11 340974 5

HOME OFFICE RESEARCH STUDIES

'Home Office Research Studies' comprise reports on research undertaken in the Home Office to assist in the exercise of its administrative functions, and for the information of the judicature, the services for which the Home Secretary has responsibility (direct or indirect) and the general public.

On the last pages of this report are listed titles already published in this series, in the preceding series *Studies in the Causes of Delinquency and the Treatment of Offenders*, and in the series of *Research and Planning Unit Papers*.

Her Majesty's Stationery Office

Standing order service

Placing a standing order with HMSO BOOKS enables a customer to receive other titles in this series automatically as published.

This saves time, trouble and expense of placing individual orders and avoids the problem of knowing when to do so.

For details please write to HMSO BOOKS (PC13A/1), Publications Centre, PO Box 276, London SW8 5DT and quoting reference X25.08.07.

The standing order service also enables customers to receive automatically as published all material of their choice which additionally saves extensive catalogue research. The scope and selectivity of the service has been extended by new techniques, and there are more than 3,500 classifications to choose from. A special leaflet describing the service in detail may be obtained on request.

Foreword

Concern about the position of the victim in the criminal justice system has increased considerably in recent years. Such concern has given rise to increased efforts on behalf of all the agencies that come into contact with victims to take into consideration victims' needs and to attempt to respond to them. This study focuses primarily on victims' informational 'needs' and, in particular on the role that police forces play in meeting them. The report does not assume that the police have sole or even primary responsibility in this area, but merely reflects the fact that it is generally the police with whom victims of crime come into contact most frequently. The report looks both at the provision of information about the progress and outcome of the case and information about the services available to victims, such as compensation and Victim Support. It concludes by considering possible improvements to the current arrangements for information provision.

MARY TUCK
Head of the Research and Planning Unit

Acknowledgements

We are very grateful to the two police forces that helped us with this research and, in particular, to the officers who bore the brunt of our requests for assistance and information: Chief Inspector Paul Anthony, Detective Chief Inspector Ray Hussey and Inspector Mick Morley. Thanks are due to all the members of the public who gave up their time to be interviewed, often to relate incidents that they would have preferred to forget. We would also like to thank Gavin Aarvold, Brian Carroll, Alan Doughty, Tony Marshall, Mike Maguire, John Pointing, Helen Reeves, Justin Russell, Dr Lorna Smith and Christine Sparke, all of whom helped us at some stage in this research.

TIM NEWBURN
SUSAN MERRY

Contents

1 Introduction

Interest in the role of victims in the criminal justice system has increased enormously in the last two decades. Although this interest has resulted in a number of developments—the expansion of court-ordered and state-funded compensation for victims, the growth of victim support—which are almost unanimously viewed as being of benefit to victims, there remain numerous areas where, it is argued, the lot of the victim is not a happy one (cf. *inter alia* Shapland *et al.*, 1985; Maguire and Corbett, 1987). Thus, for example, a Working Party was recently set up by the National Association of Victims Support Schemes to consider the role of the victim/witness in court (NAVSS, 1988). This Working Party not only recommended that courts should reconsider their practices with regard to the treatment of victims, but also recommended that:

> a procedure should be agreed by the relevant agencies in every police area to ensure that victims of crime can rely on being informed:
>
> (a) that a suspect has been charged;
>
> (b) if a decision is taken to terminate enquiries, to caution an offender, or not to proceed with a prosecution; and
>
> (c) of the date and time of the trial and the result of the case.

Such recommendations reiterate the advice contained in Home Office circular 20/1988 to Chief Police Officers. This pointed out the benefits to be gained "both for the welfare of the victim and for the police-public relationship, from making a purposeful effort to provide victims with information about progress".

The difficulties that some victims of crime experience in eliciting information about 'their' cases from agencies such as the police and the courts have also been noted in previous research (Burns-Howell *et al.*, 1982; Howley, 1982; Maguire, 1982; Shapland *et al.*, 1985; Newburn, 1988). Shapland *et al.* (1985), in a longitudinal study of the experiences of victims in the criminal justice system, charted continuous decline in levels of reported satisfaction as the victims progressed through the system. The victims in that study appeared to have been generally happy with initial contacts they had with the police but, as their cases continued, they became increasingly frustrated with the opacity of the system. Crucial to this feeling were the difficulties they encountered trying to keep in touch with developments in their cases. For example, they were almost as likely to find out whether or not the offender was on bail or in custody and what charges had actually been brought from the local newspaper as from the police themselves. Shapland et al. (1985) concluded that victims occupy a somewhat ambiguous role. On the one hand, they argued, victims are vital to the police during the recording, detection and investigation of the case, and yet on the other hand victims' experiences appeared to suggest that the police did not seem concerned to inform or consult them frequently enough, or to treat them with sufficient dignity or respect.

This research study differs from previous research in this area in a number of important respects. Firstly, it covers victims of a wider variety of offences than the study undertaken by Shapland et al. (1985), which concentrated only on victims of violent crime, and those of Burns-Howell et al. (1982) and Howley (1982), both of which concentrated on victims of property offences—mainly burglary. Secondly, as suggested above, if differs from Shapland et al.'s (1985) study in that it aims to provide only a 'snapshot' picture of the current situation rather than charting changes in attitudes through a longitudinal study. It also differs from all these studies in that it is more narrowly focused on the flow of information between police and victims rather than encompassing other parts of the criminal justice system. But, finally, it is in another sense broader than the major piece of research in this area—that of Shapland et al. (1985)—in that it looks at police–victim liaison not only from the point of view of victims, but also considers the relationship from the police standpoint.

The study consisted of semi-structured interviews with both police officers and victims in two police force areas. The sample of police officers comprised 25 officers from a single station in each area. Of the 50 officers interviewed, 35 were uniformed PCs (including six resident or home beat officers) and 15 were either Detective Constables or Detective Sergeants. Officers were asked questions designed to assess what they saw to be their general role with regard to victims of crime; to discover what types of information were regularly passed on to victims; and to investigate the extent to which police officers possessed accurate information about the services available to victims, eg. compensation and victim support.

The sample of victims was drawn from police records in the same two stations and comprised people who had reported crimes to the police within the previous year (mid-1986 to mid-1987) and whose cases were now closed, ie. either an offender had been arrested or no further investigations were taking place. Victims from all the major offence categories (excluding rape and other sexual assault) were included (see Table 1), and the cases also varied from those in which no offender had been apprehended to those which had ended with a conviction in a magistrates' or Crown Court.

Letters which explained the nature of the research and invited participation in the study were then sent with a covering letter from the police to a sample of 210 victims. In all, 100 victims were interviewed: 50 in each of the two areas, representing a response rate of approximately 48 per cent; 69 victims were men and 31 women.

Table 1

Sex of victims and type of offence

	Offence				
	Criminal damage	Theft	Burglary	Assault	Total
Men	15	18	20	16	69
Women	7	3	16	5	31
Total	22	21	36	21	100

As has already been suggested this project focuses on information-provision with the aim of identifying gaps in such provision and considering why such gaps exist and how they might be overcome. Two basic types of information that the police might be expected to pass on to victims can be identified. Firstly, there is information relating to the case itself, such as whether an arrest has been made, what charges are being made, what the outcome was and so on. Secondly, there is information about services that the victim may be entitled to or may wish to use, such as Victim Support (though victims will not usually be informed of VS directly) court-ordered compensation and the Criminal Injuries Compensation Scheme (CICS). This study considered both these areas and identified problems of provision in each.

2 Reporting the offence

Numerous other studies have highlighted the importance of victims and witnesses in the reporting of offences to the police (Mawby, 1979; Chambers and Millar, 1983, Shapland *et al.*, 1985). This was also confirmed by the findings of this study. Of the 100 victims, 64 contacted the police themselves. In a further nine cases the offence was reported by another member of the victim's household and in 11 cases by a neighbour. The remaining 16 offences were reported in the following ways: seven by people at the scene of the crime (road sweeper, bus conductor, etc); six by a colleague or other person at work; two by the offenders[1] and the remaining one by a hospital. By contrast, in only two cases did the victim say that the police 'discovered' the offence; that is, they were either on or near the scene at the time of the incident.

According to the victims' accounts, 55 per cent of the offences were reported by a telephone call to the local police station, a further 20 per cent used the 999 system and 16 per cent reported the offence in person at the local police station. In the remaining cases the offence was not reported by the victim and they did not discover how it was made known to the police. A number of studies (Shapland *et al.*, 1985; Smith and Grey, 1985) have reported that a small proportion of victims encounter difficulties with the 999 system. This was also true of a quarter of the cases in which the 999 system had been used in this study. In one case the victim had telephoned 999, waited for 20 minutes, and then rung again before the police came. In a second case, 999 had been dialled, but no police officers arrived at the scene. The victim saw and tried to stop two officers in a car who, however, said that they were unable to help as they were dealing with another case. There were 11 cases altogether in which the victim described difficulties they had experienced whilst attempting to report the offence. In three cases phone calls to the local station elicited responses which the victims described as 'unhelpful' or 'uninterested'. In one such case, in which the person was reporting that their car had been stolen, they were asked for the number and make of the car and told that:

> '. . . if it turns up we'll let you know'. And that was the end of the matter. It sounded like 'if we happen across it we'll tell you'. I didn't feel that they were going to take any real interest in it.

---

[1] In both cases the offenders had telephoned the police as they left the scene of the crime. In the more serious of the two cases, the offenders had left the victim bound and gagged in his home and had telephoned the police in order that he would be released.

5

In a further three cases victims reporting offences in person at the station felt that they were not treated with the courtesy they deserved. Two of these cases involved the theft of motor vehicles and both victims said that they were made to feel that it was their fault that the offence had occurred. One person had been stopped by the police the previous evening, breathalysed and asked to leave his vehicle parked by the side of the road whilst he accompanied the officers to the station. When he returned later to collect the vehicle he found that it had been stolen. He returned to the police station to report the offence to find, he said, that the affair was treated as 'one big joke'. He said:

> It seemed that because I was accused of drinking and driving I deserved to have my car stolen.

The other victim who experienced difficulties had a leather jacket stolen at a party. He said he expected the police to make some effort to find it, but they did not take it seriously and said to him, 'maybe it'll be handed in as lost property'. Although the majority of victims said that they had experienced no problems when reporting offences, nevertheless, a significant minority— approximately a fifth—felt that the service provided did not meet their expectations. The major reason for this feeling of dissatisfaction appeared to be the time taken and the interest shown by the officer involved in the case. Several victims complained that although the officer was courteous and appeared interested they did not really feel that all that could be done was being done. To an extent this ties in with police officers' own estimations of their jobs and capabilities. As will be discussed in more detail below, officers in general complained that because of lack of time they were not always able to deal with cases in the way that they would like.

Why do people report offences to the police? All the offences in this study were recorded by the police as crimes. As was seen above, not all the offences were reported to the police by the victim themselves. On many occasions this was undoubtedly for practical reasons (eg not being first at the scene), but, taking the results of other studies (Sparks *et al.*, 1977; Hough and Mayhew, 1983; Smith and Grey, 1985) into account, it is fair to assume that not all the victims in the sample would have reported 'their' offence to the police. There are many reasons why this may happen. Victims may view the offence as being too trivial and consequently as not being worth reporting and they may not even view themselves as a 'victim'. Interestingly, the results of this study suggest that many victims report offences to the police *despite* the fact that they may view the offence as trivial and do not perceive themselves as a victim. Although many victims said that they did not feel that the offence was particularly important, and that they had not been particularly upset by it, they still regarded it as important that it should be reported.

Thus, whereas just under a quarter of the victims singled out catching the offender as the most important reason for reporting the offence, two-fifths of

Table 2

Principal reason given for reporting offence to the police

	Number of victims
To catch the offender	23
To help the police help others	21
Its the right thing to do	19
Needed help	16
To report the loss/insurance purposes	15
Other	6
Total	100

the victims—those in the second and third categories in Table 2—said that they appreciated that there was little that the police could be expected to do but felt that it was, nevertheless, important that the offence be reported. Two major reasons were given for this. Firstly, one-fifth of victims said that they felt that by reporting the offence they might help others, either by prompting the police to be more vigilant in their area or by increasing the sum of information available to the police and indirectly enabling offenders to be apprehended. In a similar vein, a further fifth of the victims in the sample said that they reported the offence simply because they thought it was the right thing to do, it was their 'duty'. In summary, the data from this study tend to support the general conclusions from other research which point to the crucial role that victims play in reporting crime to the police. Despite often viewing offences as trivial, victims continue to believe that it is important to report offences, even though in many cases they expect to get no personal advantage from doing so.

3 First contact between police and victim

Police officers' perceptions of initial contacts with victims

Officers were asked a number of questions about the nature of the first visit to the scene of a crime or contact with a victim. The questions were directed towards discovering what type of information was routinely passed on to victims on the first occasion they came into contact with the police. Police officers interviewed by Shapland *et al.* (1985) agreed that such occasions were directed towards discovering what essentially had happened and the nature of the victim's complaint. The officers in this study tended to argue along similar lines, namely, that the first meeting was an opportunity to get information *from* the victim, rather than to give it. The primary task was identified as being to take the details of what had happened, and then to tell the 'injured party' that inquiries would be made. Statements such as 'running the victim through the stages of the inquiry', or 'giving an insight into how the investigation will proceed' were used by over a third of the officers in describing what they considered to be the best way of involving the victim and making them feel a part of what was going on.

Many officers suggested that the promise of a follow-up visit from the Scenes of Crime Officer (SOCO) or the Crime Prevention Officer (CPO)—particularly in burglary cases—could also be used to assure the victim that something was being done on their behalf. However, almost all officers complained of lack of time and said that they were generally unable to make follow-up visits themselves. This was slightly different for beat officers who felt that they had more time than their colleagues to make follow-up visits and, because they worked in one 'patch', they were more frequently in the area and therefore able to call on the victim. Consequently, Resident Beat Officers (RBOs) suggested that they were much more likely to re-visit victims than many of their colleagues. Beat officers were also compared by some to officers who worked in rural areas. As one police officer said:

> Very few IPs (injured parties) need further contact even though to them its a major thing in their lives, to us it happens 100 times a day. Different in a village where you do chat, its no problem to pop in. In town we tend to wait for them to contact us.

The necessity for a follow-up visit was generally seen to be determined by police requirements—for example, the need for information—rather than victims' needs. When asked on what basis decisions about whether to pay a second visit were made, most officers' answers revolved around the need to ask more questions, to take a statement, make arrangements for identification parades, viewing of photographs, etc.

Although police officers generally were in favour of keeping victims informed of developments in cases, they suggested that this was frequently impractical because of lack of time. They thought that in many cases the most they could be expected to do at the initial meeting would be to describe to the victim how things would proceed, and to tell them to get in touch if there was anything else that they required. Almost all officers said that they felt that victims would expect to be informed of the outcome of a case in which no offenders had been apprehended. However, a sixth of those interviewed stated categorically that they would not inform victims under such circumstances. A further tenth said that, when appropriate, they would tell victims during the first contact that there was little chance of an arrest being made and, having done so, would treat this as having informed the victim of the outcome of the case. In one force officers were required to tick a box on the crime report to indicate that they had told the victim the result of their investigations. It was said that this would on occasion be done during the first visit.

Officers were asked if, during this first contact, they gave victims their name and a telephone number at which they could be contacted. All the officers in the sample said that they did and most said that they would write this information down. The CID officers and some of the beat officers in one area had cards (some officially produced and some privately) with their name, rank, number and the name and address of the police station printed on it. The officers who possessed such cards said that they were useful, although a minority of the officers who did not have them but knew of their use were somewhat sceptical. On the one hand some argued that cards seemed rather too formal, one officer commenting 'we're not insurance agents!', and on the other hand, it was felt that calling cards could be passed off as warrant cards by people wishing to impersonate police officers.

The reasons given for telling victims where and how the officer could be contacted were of two main types. The most frequently cited reason was so that any further information that came to light could be passed on to the police. Several officers said that victims were often too upset to remember things in detail on the first occasion, and they often rang up to provide further pieces of information a day or two after the offence. The second major reason given was to enable victims to inquire about what was happening in their case. The officers suggested that the most frequent type of inquiry that they received was that concerning whether property had been recovered. No officers reported ever having had victims contact them in order to ask for advice about what was likely to happen in court, how they could apply for, or whether they were likely to receive, compensation, how to contact a victim support scheme, etc, etc.

10

Victims' perceptions of initial contacts with the police

As was suggested above, the police officers in the study suggested that the initial contact with victims was dominated by the organisational need to secure information rather than to provide information for the victim. They further argued that the major constraint upon them was time, and that the lack of time available to them to spend with victims meant that there were obvious limits to the service they could therefore provide. Given this stress on time victims were asked to estimate how long their initial contact with the police lasted. Fifty-eight per cent estimated less than half an hour, 21 per cent between half an hour and an hour, nine per cent at over one hour and 12 per cent did not know. The circumstances of the first meeting varied depending on the nature of the offence and the method by which the offence was reported. The majority of victims (55 per cent) first came into contact with the police at the scene of the crime, 23 per cent at the police station, a further 17 per cent were visited at home (where this wasn't the scene of the crime), two per cent were visited in hospital and three per cent could not remember where the first meeting took place. Over 90 per cent of victims had their initial contact with one or more uniformed officers, the rest with CID. None of the victims expressed any strong feelings about the venue of their first contact with the police; there were neither any major expressions of dissatisfaction nor any explicit thoughts about how the contact might have been improved.

Both Burns-Howell *et al.* (1982) and Howley, (1982), found that during the first contact the majority of victims expected the police to follow established procedures and decide upon what further action needed to be taken. This general finding was again largely confirmed by this study. Over half of the victims interviewed said that they merely expected the police to come and ask them questions and take down all the relevant details of the case. This it appears is a realistic estimate of what is likely to happen. Over 70 per cent of the victims in this study reported that the police had spent most of the time asking for information, questioning witnesses, searching the house or the scene of the crime, whereas only eight per cent could remember being given a specific piece of information themselves by the police. The remainder either stressed other activities or could not clearly remember what the police had done. Although just under a quarter of the victims interviewed said that catching the offender was the most important reason why they reported the offence to the police, when asked what they expected the police to do in response to their having reported the offence, one-third said 'catch the offender'.

Victims were asked if, during this initial contact, the police said that they would do anything further, or suggested that the victim should do something. Table 3 below sets out the major courses of action that the victims reported the police mentioning. Only just over half the victims could remember an officer mentioning such further action.

11

Table 3

Further action mentioned by the police on initial visit

| | Police force | | |
Action	Area 1	Area 2	Total
SOCO* would call	6	11	17
Would pass case to CID	4	7	11
Would be a follow-up call	2	7	9
Would contact again if any result	3	4	7
Would help with insurance	1	2	3
Would help with or advise on repairs	1	1	2
Would send CPO†	0	1	1
Advised hospital treatment	0	1	1
Total	17	34	51

* SOCO: Scenes of crime officer.

† CPO: Crime prevention officer.

Despite the unanimously positive response of police officers in this study to the question about whether they gave their name and a telephone number where the victim could contact them, less than two-thirds of victims reported that this had happened. In one of the areas just over half of those interviewed said that they had been given such information compared with just over two-thirds in the other. Although overall, over three-fifths of victims were provided with the means by which they could contact an officer dealing with their case, as will be discussed in chapter 4, few victims made use of this facility. Many victims, of course, either do not require or do not perceive a need to use such a facility. However, the reasons for providing a telephone number with which to contact the officer on the case appeared not have been fully explained to some victims. Although the majority understood that they were to get in touch if they had more information that might be of use to the police, less than half seemed to have been told that they should ring if there was more that *they* needed or if they wished to find out what was happening in the case. This disparity again highlights the dominance of operational requirements over victims' needs—just as more priority appears to be given to police, rather than victims', informational needs during initial contacts, explanations given by officers about the necessity and possibility of future contact also seem to stress police requirements.

On the basis of interviews with police officers, Burns-Howell *et al.* (1982) concluded that whilst police officers may often believe crimes are unlikely to be detected, they would rarely tell victims this. The data from this study suggest just the opposite. In fact, the one piece of information that was given with regularity during the first contact with the victim was the officers' perception of the likelihood of tracing an offender. In over two-thirds of cases victims were given such information and in a further 12 per cent the victim was aware the offender had already been arrested. None of the victims interviewed expressed any reservations about being given such information in the early stages of the case, eg. at the first contact, even when the officer had said quite bluntly that the chances of an arrest were almost non-existent. Victims appeared much more likely to be realistic rather than optimistic about clear-up rates. Informing victims of the limited chances of an arrest being made was *not* a source of dissatisfaction with the police: realism was accepted. Resentment *was* caused, however, when officers gave an impression of apathy, of not seeming to care. The victims in this study appeared to find it easier when an officer gave a realistic estimate of what they thought would be the likely outcome even if this involved the suggestion that the chances of arrest were minimal and further contact with the police probably unnecessary.

Although attempting to measure 'customer' satisfaction with services is inherently problematic (Ekblom and Heal, 1982), responses to survey questions about satisfaction can at least be taken as an indication of the degree to which expectations are met. When asked to describe their expectations the majority of victims concentrated upon *what* they expected the police to do, and *how* they expected them to do it. The most common descriptions given by victims in this study were that the police had been 'concerned', 'sympathetic' or 'considerate'. Victims frequently said that they had looked for general reassurance or support from the police during what was for them a worrying time. One couple who described themselves as 'very satisfied' with the way they had been treated said that the officer who had first contacted them had been very supportive and had 'put us at ease as soon as he came in'. Other comments from those who were very satisfied included:

He seemed very concerned, he couldn't have been nicer.

They were excellent: patient, kind and understanding. They did everything they could.

Victims were asked to rate their degree of satisfaction on a five point scale from very satisfied to very dissatisfied. In both areas 40 per cent of victims said that they were very satisfied with their initial contact with the police. Forty-four per cent in one area and 46 per cent in the other said that they were satisfied. Overall, 85 per cent of the victims in this study said they were satisfied or very satisfied with the police during their initial contact. When asked to explain why this was, the majority of victims described the attitude or behaviour of the officers they met. This is very much in line with Shapland *et al.*'s (1985) finding that victims' satisfaction with their initial meeting with the police, was mainly due to 'the manner of the police, the speed at which the police came and whether the police were seen to do what the victim expected they would do'.

Only a small proportion of the victims interviewed reported being dissatisfied or very dissatisfied after their first contact with the police. Five per cent of victims described themselves as dissatisfied and three per cent as very dissatisfied. Dissatisfaction appeared to be related to the same factors as satisfaction. That is, as with other studies (Maguire, 1982; Jones, 1983; Shapland et al., 1985), it was those victims who felt that the police officers were not taking their case seriously, or were not sympathetic or considerate who reported dissatisfaction. It was the *demeanour* of the police rather than some other technical or investigative matter that appeared to be crucial. In one such case a man's car had been damaged at night whilst it was parked outside his house. He discovered it in the morning long after, he assumed, the incident had occurred. The police took a look at the car, noted a few details, told him that there was little they could do and left. He lived in a small village and made his own inquiries, asking people if they had seen or heard anything and discovered that another car had been damaged on the same evening. In his explanation of his dissatisfaction with the police he said that it was not that no-one had been apprehended, but that he had the impression that the police were not going to attempt to make any inquiries regarding the offence. Extreme dissatisfaction was reported by another person who had had his motorbike stolen. Again, he appreciated that there was probably little that the police could do as far as catching the offender was concerned, but he felt that they were not even interested in finding the stolen bike. He said:

> All they were concerned about was getting away as quickly as possible. They didn't seem to care. In future I'd take my business elsewhere if I could.

In summary, well over four-fifths of the victims in this study expressed satisfaction with the way they were treated by the police during their initial contact. Many of these respondents described the police as helpful, considerate, sympathetic or patient.

However, as was suggested above, ratings of satisfaction can't be understood without reference to expectations. It was clear during many interviews that the victims did not have high expectations of what could be achieved by the police. In cases of domestic burglary, criminal damage and theft of motor vehicles, most victims appreciated that clear-up rates were low and that detection was by no means guaranteed. By and large, the police confirmed such feelings when they gave the victim their assessment of the possibility of an arrest being made. Under such circumstances, where it is widely accepted that detection, arrest and prosecution are relatively uncommon, it is the attitude of the police attending the scene of the crime, or making the first contact with the victim, that appears to be crucial in determining the degree to which the victim is satisfied with the service they receive. Those who expressed dissatisfaction with the conduct of their initial meeting with the police, and this was less than one-tenth of those interviewed, cited the lack of attention, sympathy or concern that was shown by the police as being the major reason for their dissatisfaction.

Finally, to what extent did the initial contact between the police and the victim lead to any inconvenience for the latter? Shapland et al. (1985), reported that 22 per cent of their sample had experienced some inconvenience as a result of this initial contact with the police. Only 11 out of the 100 victims interviewed as part of this study reported being inconvenienced in some way. These victims reported having to take time off work, arrange carers for their children, having to cancel appointments etc. The higher rate reported by Shapland *et al.* (1985) is probably to be explained by the rather more serious offences suffered by the victims in their sample, and consequently the increased demands upon their time made by the police. Unlike Shapland *et al.* (1985), only one of the victims in this study who was inconvenienced linked that inconvenience with feelings of dissatisfaction at the conduct of the initial meeting. The nature of the inconvenience most usually involved such things as taking time off work in order to be at home or to visit the police station. There was also one victim who was self-employed who had had to cancel appointments. All of those who reported inconvenience, however, appeared to be fairly phlegmatic about the wasted time, few were concerned about it, and only one such victim reported being dissatisfied with the initial contact with the police.

4 Keeping in touch with developments in the case

The findings presented in chapter 3 confirmed those of studies such as that of Shapland *et al.* (1985) in which victims' experiences of initial contacts with the police were described as being fairly positive, with police officers viewed as largely helpful and courteous. Shapland *et al.* (1985) went on to argue, however, that victims' satisfaction with their contacts with the police declined from this point onwards, and that, furthermore, this decline in satisfaction was in large measure due to the difficulties victims experienced in obtaining information about developments in their cases. This study, therefore, paid particular attention to victims' experiences of the availability of case-status information: the major question considered was whether there are specific pieces or types of information which victims suggest that they would like to be given, but which appear not to be being communicated to them on a regular or systematic basis?

Subsequent contacts between the victim and the police

One-third of the victims in the sample had no contact with the police other than that immediately after the offence had been reported. Among those who did have subsequent contacts there was considerable variation in terms of the number of such contacts, the reasons for further communication and who the contact had been initiated by (this is summarised in Table 4). Such variation

Table 4

Reasons for further contact between police and victim

Reason for contact	Number of occasions
Further information (for the police)	36
Further information (for the victim—police initiated contact)	
information about arrest	32
other general information	17
Further information (for the victim—victim initiated contact)	10*
Visit by SOCO	25
Take statement	10
Other	4

* This figure represents the number of victims making contact with the police for information. The number of such contacts was not known.

E

was largely determined by the nature of the case. Most of the subsequent contacts between the victim and the police occurred within a few days of the offence being reported and the majority (75 per cent) were either for police informational purposes or were related to other aspects of police procedure. As Burns-Howell *et al.* (1982) noted:

> . . . the public are left with the impression that such further contact has been police initiated because of a need to satisfy some bureaucratic need or routine.

As will become clear from the more detailed discussion of victim informational needs below, much of the positive work done by the police in the hours and days after the offence was first reported was undone in the eyes of the victim by the lack of contact as the case progressed.

The need for more information was the most common reason for further contact between the victim and the police. This was of two sorts: either the police passing on information to the victim or attempting to obtain further information themselves. When the police passed on information, it generally involved details of the case, concerning, for example, the recovery of property, having made an arrest, whether charges were being brought, asking about dates for court, etc. On a total of 36 occasions the police contacted the victim in order to make further inquiries, on 32 occasions to pass on information about an arrest and on a further 17 occasions in order to pass on other pieces of more general information about the progress of the case. Ten of the victims in the sample made contact with the police in order to request further information, some 'phoning the police on five or more occasions.

In 25 cases the victim was visited by the Scenes of Crime Officer (SOCO). One victim reported that she had an appointment with the SOCO, but that the officer did not keep the appointment. All but four of the victims were content with their dealings with the SOCO, many finding the officer's attempts at gathering evidence reassuring. On one occasion, however, the officer arrived in order to make casts of footprints outside the scene of a burglary. Having done the job, he left the casts in the front garden and never returned to collect them. The victim was still able to produce them when the researcher called to conduct the interview. The other three victims reported having to wait a long time for the SOCO to arrive.

Although there were 36 burglaries in the sample, only five victims were visited by the Crime Prevention Officer (CPO). These five had found the advice they received useful and reassuring. A number of victims, however, said that they would have liked crime prevention advice but that it had not been offered and that they did not know how to arrange for the officer to visit. One couple, who had been burgled twice in the preceding year and had also had their mail tampered with, had rung the police station to try to arrange for the CPO to call round. They were told that there was only one CPO and that he only worked from 8 am to 5 pm. As they were both out during the day themselves it was consequently not possible for the CPO to call round at a time that was convenient for them. They felt that they were not only being denied advice and help with securing their home, but were also being denied the peace of mind that they thought would come as a result of having attempted to do all they could to prevent future victimisation.

The outcome of the inquiries

For many of the victims interviewed in this study, the crucial pieces of information that they wished to know concerned whether or not an offender had been arrested and, if so, what the outcome of any proceedings were. The results of the study suggest that whilst the police tend to inform victims when an arrest is made they are much less likely to let them know the final outcome in the case. In almost half of the cases in the sample an arrest was made. Of the 46 arrests, eight occurred at or around the scene of the crime and the victim was present or in the vicinity when the arrest was made. In 32 of the remaining 38 cases, in which an arrest was made at a later stage, the victims were informed by the police that an arrest had been made. In one of these cases the police had been the source of the information but the victim had had to telephone in order to find out. However, generally speaking, where an arrest had been made the victim was usually informed that this had occurred. In the six cases in which the victim did not find out about the arrest from the police, three found out from friends, one from the newspaper, one from the local victim support scheme and one found out because his son was a police officer. It was, however, after the stage at which an arrest had been made that the information flow between the police and victims appeared to dry up.

As was suggested above, although information about arrest was consistently passed on to victims, the flow of information about the outcome of inquiries— whether or not charges were being made, the sentence of the court, etc— appeared to be somewhat more problematic. Thirty-one of the 100 victims said that they had been told by the police what the outcome of their inquiries had been. In only a minority of these cases did the police inform the victim of the sentence of the court. A number of victims had made inquiries themselves but without success. Perhaps more illuminating in this context were the *expectations* victims held. Although, as has been suggested, most victims *wanted* to be informed of the outcome of the case and, indeed, 68 per cent of victims said that they thought that they *should* have been informed by the police—irrespective of whether an arrest had been made— only 55 per cent said that they *expected* to be informed. Of those who did not think that it was necessary for the police to keep them informed, many felt this was because their particular case was too trivial for the police to spend much time on. This was a recurrent theme running through interviews with many victims; irrespective of whether they had been kept informed or not. There appeared to be a sense in which they felt that they were wasting police time. There were others who were more needy than themselves and therefore they couldn't expect the police to treat their case as a priority. Only rarely did a victim describe themselves as 'needy' or suggest that their needs were important.

Despite this denial, however, victims continued to express a desire for information about certain aspects of their case.

What happened to the offender

One such area on which information was desired was that concerning the offender. Finding out what happened to the offender was described as being very important by most victims. It was the signal for them that the case had been officially closed. Without such information victims said that they had to make assumptions about what had or was happening, and they were left without the security of knowing that the incident was over.

In only 27 of the 46 cases (59 per cent) in which an arrest had been made did the victim know what had happened to the offender. Of these 27, 16 had either been in court or were informed by the police. Five heard by word of mouth, three by reading the local press, one from a victim support scheme and two discovered what at least part of the sentence was when they received a letter from the court telling them that they had been awarded compensation.

Those victims who had not heard what had happened to the offender said unanimously that they would like to know, and would have liked to have been informed by the police. Some still harboured hopes that they would still be so informed. Although many victims had been supplied with the name of an officer to contact and a phone number to ring, relatively few took advantage of this. In all, 40 of the victims in the sample said that they would have liked more information about the progress or the outcome of the case, but only 10 contacted the police themselves. A number explained this reticence by suggesting that they did not realise that they would be able to ask for information about the case. This was particularly evident once the case had got to court. When this had occurred victims were unsure who would have the information they required. Those who did ring the police usually met with little success. Of the 10 who did make enquiries, seven said that they received a negative and unhelpful response. As did those in Howley's (1982) sample, victims in this study frequently found it difficult to contact the officer they believed to be dealing with their case by telephone, and when visiting the station personally, reported great difficulty in getting relevant information from the officer on the desk. Having attempted to make inquiries, victims then expected the police to contact them when information became available: again, this rarely happened.

It has been stated earlier that the greatest informational desire on the part of victims was to be informed about the ending of inquiries or the sentence of the court. This was expressed in several different ways. All were, however, linked by the desire to know the outcome of the case, so that the experience can in some sense be regarded as closed. The first reason given by victims for wishing to be kept informed was that if they were not told then all they could do was assume that nothing had happened:

I think they should say something, even if its just to say nothing happened.

Having not heard from the police, all I can assume is that no-one was apprehended.

When you hear nothing (*sic*), all you can assume is that they just don't care.

The second reason given by victims for wanting to be kept informed was in order to relieve their nerves or bad feelings about the offence:

I wanted to be informed about what had happened. I was a nervous wreck and it would have helped.

The incident left me feeling terrible. I was shaky and nervous for a long time. I would have liked to have been told what was going on.

Thirdly, victims liked being kept informed to maintain the level of their confidence with the police. Providing information was viewed as an integral part of police activities and, consequently, as far as many victims were concerned, if they were not receiving information then the police were not doing their job properly:

I never heard. It felt like they weren't going to do anything. They should have let us know.

No, they didn't tell me what happened, and it's bloody atrocious. They (the offenders) could be walking the streets for all I know.

I'd have certainly wanted to know what happened if it had been more serious. It assures you that they (the police) are thinking about it and taking care.

The above quote also contains the already mentioned feeling that victims often expressed that their case was not really very serious, and that, therefore, they were not really surprised that they were not kept informed about the status of their case.

Finally, some victims felt that despite the effort they had put into the case (reporting, answering questions, going to the police station, court, etc) they were not rewarded with similar effort from the police:

You're put off slightly if nothing happens. It's as if they don't appreciate that you've tried to help them. It's like work. If you're never told you've done well, then you start to give up after a while.

The data from this study suggest that victims want to be kept informed. They also tend to feel that the responsibility for keeping them informed rests with the police—though it is worth remembering that this is probably explained by the fact that the police are the victims' only early source of information. When their informational expectations were not met they felt let down. Of the victims in the study who complained that they had not been provided with as much information on the progress of the case as they would have liked, the majority were mainly concerned with the outcome of the case. There were isolated examples where the victim had been worried by their lack of knowledge about other aspects of the case eg. whether the offender had been granted bail, when an offender given a custodial sentence would be released etc. However, the one piece of information that was required above all others was the outcome of the case. Victims wanted to be informed when enquiries had come to an end, when for instance charges were not being made (and why not) or what the sentence was if the case got as far as court.

Problems with information flow

Given such a clearly expressed desire it is worth exploring at this point why such information is not regularly and routinely supplied for victims. As was suggested in chapter 3, police officers argued that follow-up visits would tend to be made on those occasions when the *police* required further information, rather than on occasions when there was new information of relevance to the *victim*. Officers were asked a number of questions about the handling of cases; what case-status information was available to them, and whether they found it easy to keep victims informed and up-to-date. Although in both forces officers had access to information on most aspects of the cases they were dealing with, the way in which crime reports and related papers were handled created difficulties for individual officers. In both areas the major problems associated with providing information for victims came in cases which reached court. Thus, although officers would almost always be able to inform victims of the apprehension and charging of an offender, as well as the date of the first court hearing, at this point their direct contact with the case and, therefore, their ability to keep in touch with developments, ended.

In most cases, officers said that they would try to let the victim know that an offender had been apprehended. They pointed out that such information would certainly be passed on in a proportion of cases as the taking of a statement is sometimes left until an arrest is made. In such cases, therefore, the arrest would necessitate further contact between police and victim. Problems arise, however, if cases are serious enough to be passed to the CID. Uniformed officers argued that when this occurred they ceased to have any significant involvement in the case and would not be able to ensure that information was passed to the victim. The CID officers interviewed said that they could not always be sure in such cases what information had already been passed on and what had not.

Organisations such as Victim Support have stressed that all victims should be given the opportunity to be present in court whether or not they are required as a witness. In order that this is possible all victims would need to be informed of the dates of court hearings. The data from this research suggest that in those cases where there is an arrest, charges made and a not guilty plea entered, the victim would automatically be sent a letter telling them that they might be required as a witness in court and informing them of the date of the hearing. However, in cases where there is a guilty plea and a witness is unlikely to be required, all officers said that victims would not automatically be informed of court dates. This general procedure was confirmed by the officer in charge of the prosecutions section at one of the stations—and, therefore, responsible for witness letters—who said:

> We don't deal with victims, at least we don't think of them as victims, we deal with witnesses.

The fact that the victim was not likely to be required in court meant that they were not routinely informed of the fact that the case was going to court. Some officers did suggest that, when they were able to, they would generally let the victim know the date of the first court hearing but thereafter they would not be able to keep the victim informed. Officers complained that since the introduction of the Crown Prosecution Service (CPS) they had far less information about what was happening at court and, consequently, less opportunity to help victims at court. This situation also meant that one very important piece of information was not readily available to the police, and therefore was not passed on by them to victims; the result of court proceedings. Although the result of the case is passed back to the police by the CPS, in the two areas studied this was taking up to two months. The majority of police officers interviewed suggested that this was generally long past the point where they were able to keep track of all the cases in which they had been involved. Furthermore, they argued that most victims who wanted to know the result of their cases would have found out by other means such as the local press. In this aspect, as in others, the onus was once again on the victim. If they made inquiries then, it was argued, they would be likely to be able to discover from the police what had happened to 'their' case. However, if they were not at court (even if they knew when the case was to be held) they were only likely to be informed of the result after considerable delay, if at all. The police were frequently unable to supply such information either because it was unavailable to them, or because it was only available a considerable time after they had ceased to be involved in the case.

The general position appears to be one in which there is a general desire on the part of victims for certain specific types of information—particularly those concerning the outcome of the case. There also appears to be at least a partial recognition by the police that such information should be passed on to victims, but that this is qualified by the logistics of police organisation. Thus, the police argue that they are constrained by limited resources, particularly by lack of time, and that whilst they might wish to keep all victims informed about the outcome of their cases it is not always possible. They further argue that the criminal justice system is organised in such a way, particularly since the introduction of the Crown Prosecution Service, that information about the sentence of the court often only reaches them after some, occasionally considerable, delay.

5 Information about services for victims

Two basic types of information that the police might be expected to pass on to victims were identified in chapter 1. There is, firstly, information relating to the progress of the case and, secondly, there is information about services that are, or may be, available to victims of crime. The latter may be divided into three basic areas: information about the Criminal Injuries Compensation Scheme (CICS), information about compensation from the criminal courts and information about Victim Support. This chapter examines information-provision in all these areas.

A number of authors (Miers, 1978; Shapland *et al.*, 1985) have expressed doubts about the frequency with which victims are informed about the availability of compensation. That the importance of such information is recognised is illustrated by the publication of Home Office circular 20/1988 which reinforced the advice contained in previous circulars (143/1979 and 27/1983) that victims of violent crime should be made aware of the existence of the CICS and of the possibility of compensation from the criminal courts. With regard to the CICS, the circular stated that 'it remains important that police officers, who in the vast majority of cases are the first to come into contact with victims of violent crime, should bring the Scheme to victim's attention'. It was suggested in the circular that to aid this process victims should be provided with a copy of the leaflet 'Victims of Crimes of Violence—A Guide to the Criminal Injuries Compensation Scheme'.

The 50 police officers interviewed in this study were asked whether they generally advised all victims of the existence of compensation for injury from the CICS. Depending on their answer they were also asked which victims were or were not informed, and the nature of the information given. In order to check the degree to which officers were in possession of accurate information about the scheme, they were also asked if they knew the current minimum financial limit operated by the Board.

Exactly half of the officers interviewed said that they did not always advise victims of the possibility of compensation from CICS. These officers could be roughly divided into two basic types; those who accepted that giving victims such information was probably their responsibility and those who felt it was not their responsibility at all. The most frequent reason given by the former group was that they did not know about or had only a little information about the

25

scheme. Several officers complained that they had not been told about such things during the course of their training, others that, although they had heard of the existence of CICS, they did not know how it worked or how to get information about it. Those who thought it was not their responsibility were either uniformed police officers who argued that informing victims about CICs should be left to CID, or felt it was not a police responsibility at all and that solicitors or other agencies generally were, or should be, the source of such information. There were 21 assault victims in the sample and of these 14 had received information about CICS and six had made claims as a result. Two of those who had made claims had received awards and the rest had not yet heard the result of their claim. Only six of the 14 victims who had been given information about the CICS said that they had been informed of its existence by the police. Four victims had been told of CICS by the local victim support scheme, two by friends, one by his solicitor and one by a hospital.

Although half the officers said that they did routinely inform victims of the existence of compensation for injury from CICS, many of them when questioned further, admitted that they did not inform *all* victims who had suffered injury of CICS. Such officers were, however, generally confident that they could distinguish between those who needed such information and those who did not. Two basic distinctions were operated by the police in determining which side of these boundaries particular victims should fall. These distinctions were between crimes that were or were not 'serious' enough to warrant awards from CICS, and between 'deserving' and 'non-deserving' victims. The major method of determining the seriousness of crime was by using the distinction between injuries associated with a charge of actual bodily harm (ABH) and grievous bodily harm (GBH). If a charge of GBH was viewed by the officer as being a fair reflection of the types of injuries sustained, then it was suggested that such a case would be likely to be worthy of an award from CICS and, therefore, the victim would be likely to be informed. However, if less serious charges were thought appropriate, officers argued that they would be less likely to inform the victim of the existence of the Scheme. This procedure appeared to have been used with regard to informing the victims in this study. All of those who said that the police had told them about CICS were involved in cases in which the offender was charged with GBH, and there were several cases of ABH where the victim had not been informed of the existence of CICS by the police.

The claim by officers that they are able to judge what types of injury are likely to result in awards from the Board may be viewed against their answers to the factual question about the financial minimum operated by CICS. Of the 50 officers interviewed, 22 said that they did not know what the minimum was. Of the 28 who thought they either knew or had a rough idea, only three stated the correct sum of £550. However, the limit had been raised within the last 12 months from £400, and a further 15 officers mentioned a figure somewhere between these two figures. Nevertheless, less than a quarter of the officers questioned mentioned a figure that was within £100 of the actual financial minimum used by the scheme.

The second distinction used to determine who should be given, or who was considered to need, information on criminal injuries compensation, ie the distinction between the deserving and non-deserving, was somewhat more complicated than that used to distinguish seriousness of injury. A number of authors have written about the 'ideal victim' (Christie, 1986; Miers, 1980; Shapland et al., 1985). Such a victim is distinguished by a number of important attributes which may include age, respectability, sex and the location or context in which victimisation occurred. Depending on the attributes of the particular person under consideration and the context of the victimisation, ascription of 'victim' status becomes more or less likely. Thus, in crude terms, a young male injured whilst committing a crime is far less likely to be perceived as a victim than is an elderly woman attacked on the street. The police officers in this study seemed to operate on the basis of a set of stereotyped and idealistic victim characteristics. There appeared to be an assumption in operation that there were some victims who 'could look after themselves' and, consequently, did not require much assistance from the police. On the other hand, the elderly, the infirm and, often, women living on their own were singled out as those who would be likely to require help and support. With regard to compensation, victims were divided into, for example, 'the old lady who has every right to claim' and 'local yobbos' perhaps injured in a pub fight, who 'have to sort it out for themselves'. The latter were distinguished from 'true victims' and the police suggested that the 'local yobbos' would be very unlikely to be told about facilities such as CICS.

Two of the officers in the sample had themselves made successful applications to CICS, one of whom said that he informed victims if he thought the injury was serious enough whereas the other said that he never informed victims as he rarely thought about compensation. Some officers also expressed reservations about compensation for the victims of certain types of crime, in particular, domestic assaults. These were seen as being awkward to deal with, and those involved in them were viewed by some officers as being in some way to blame for their predicament, and consequently as falling outside the category of the 'innocent victim'.

In summary, although the officers interviewed appeared to be generally unfamiliar with the exact procedures operated by CICS they had established procedures which to some extent mirrored those operated by CICS. Thus, although the CICS itself operates a financial minimum and uses a distinction between 'deserving' and 'undeserving' victims, the police themselves tended to assess the seriousness of injury and only informed those whom they felt would be likely to get an award, as well as also excluding those they viewed as 'undeserving'. Although assessing the seriousness of injury was explained by officers as being necessary because of the terms of the scheme, assessing the 'worthiness' of victims was not. This was generally presented as being a decision made by the individual officer on the basis of his or her ideas of right and wrong. Little attempt was made to justify such a procedure, but rather the limitation of compensation to 'true' victims was presented as being self-evidently necessary.

Compensation from the courts

Compensation orders may be made by both the Crown Court and magistrates' courts, and involve the payment of a specified amount of money by the offender via the court to the victim. An order may be made in respect of any victim who has suffered personal injury, loss or damage as a result of an offence. Although compensation may be awarded in a wide variety of cases, it tends to be concentrated in the major offence categories of criminal damage, theft and assault. Recent research (Newburn, 1988) has shown that compensation orders tend to be awarded far more frequently in cases in which there is material loss, ie theft, burglary and criminal damage, than in cases in which there is personal injury. That research suggested that part of the reason for this situation was that magistrates were not provided with accurate information about the extent of injury, and that claims for compensation in such cases were rarely made in court. This was the result of certain practices adopted by the police, in particular, the use by many forces of a claim form which included details of loss or damage to property but not of injury. As these forms have become the basis upon which claims are made in court by the Crown Prosecution Service, claims in injury cases are consequently comparatively rare.

One of the aims of this research, therefore, was to establish in more detail how these procedures operated and, in particular, to look at the types of information that were passed on to victims. In the same way the police seemed to lack accurate knowledge of CICS, their knowledge about which victims were eligible for compensation from the magistrates' courts or the Crown Court also appeared incomplete. Of the 50 officers interviewed, 43 said that they would inform victims in criminal damage cases of the availability of compensation from the courts, 39 said they would inform victims who had had property stolen, but only 15 said they would inform victims who had suffered injury. However, although these officers said that they would pass on such information, this did not guarantee that claims would be made on behalf of such victims in court. Three of the 15 officers who claimed to inform injured victims said that they did not make claims on the victim's behalf, one suggesting that this was the job of the Crown Prosecution Service, the other two arguing that compensation for injury was the responsibility of the court. This was despite the fact that it was the procedure in both forces to collect the necessary information, eg invoices, with which to support a claim for compensation in cases of loss of, or damage to, property. Some officers appeared to assume that providing details did not apply equally in all cases. The reasons given by officers for not informing injured victims of the availability of court compensation varied considerably. Some appeared to believe that compensation for injury was a civil matter rather than something to be considered by the criminal courts, others felt that minor injuries would not warrant compensation. Related to this was the belief expressed by a tenth of the officers interviewed that the more serious injuries were to be dealt with by CICS, and consequently claims in court were unnecessary.

Officers were also asked if they consulted victims about their desire for compensation, and whether they would wish a claim to be made on their behalf in court. Although there was an even split between those answering positively and those negatively, there appeared to be considerable confusion over what such a procedure might actually involve. In the aforementioned study of compensation orders (Newburn, 1988) a number of victims who had been awarded compensation from a court, and who were interviewed as part of the research, suggested that they were surprised when they received the first payment from the court, as they had not known that a claim had been made. This research study points to a possible explanation for this situation.

Both police forces in this study used forms on which to record details of loss and damage (and possibly injury) as well as whether or not a claim should be made for compensation. However, because filling in such details was part of the standard procedure for preparing papers for court and, therefore, something that could be done without further contact with the victim, frequently victims were not consulted about whether or not they wished to be compensated. Filling in this form, or this part of the form, was viewed very much as a routine activity to be done when a suspect had been apprehended and charged, and it was also often assumed that victims would want compensation. As one officer said, 'it's up to them to say they don't want it'. Even in cases where the victim had been asked about compensation, this was likely to have occurred at the initial stages of the inquiry and not at the point at which an arrest had been made. Thus, although a victim suffering damage to, or loss of, property would have approximately an 80 per cent chance of being informed of the possibility of compensation from a court, they would not always be asked by these officers if they wished compensation and would not always be aware in those cases where a claim had been made on their behalf.

Victims in this study were asked whether they knew of ways of claiming compensation, if so, how they had learned of them, and, finally, whether or not they had made a claim. Of the 100 cases, 24 ended with a guilty verdict in court and consequently compensation could theoretically have been ordered by the court. In practice, the courts will rarely award compensation against an offender if a custodial sentence is deemed to be appropriate (Newburn, 1988). This reduced the number of cases in which a compensation order might have been expected to 18. Of these 18, five involved a compensation order. Three of the five who had compensation awarded complained about the methods of payment. One victim said:

29

Cheques started coming, £1.50 at a time. Tiny amounts. Not worth a trip to the bank. I would have liked the court to pay me [the full sum].

All five offences which involved compensation were theft or burglary, reinforcing the point made earlier that compensation orders are rarely made for injury. In three of these five cases the victim did not know that compensation had been claimed. It simply came 'automatically' or 'out of the blue', they said. Overall, only seven of the victims in the sample said that they had been told that criminal courts could make awards of compensation.

It appears from the results of this study that, although the police may occasionally make claims for compensation on behalf of victims, they neither ensure that the victim knows that this is what is occurring, nor do they tell victims about the rules governing awards of compensation from the courts as a matter of course. The claims procedure is viewed by police officers as a largely automatic one and victims are informed only cursorily—if at all—of the procedure.

In summary, with regard to compensation orders, even when informed of the possibility of criminal compensation there appeared to be no guarantee that victims would be told whether a claim was being made on their behalf. Equally, because a significant proportion of victims were not informed of the sentence of the court, they were sometimes unaware that compensation had been awarded and were taken by surprise when the first payment arrived from the court.

Use of and attitudes towards victim support

As Maguire and Corbett (1987) have pointed out, Victim Support Schemes (VSSs) are heavily dependant upon the local police for their referrals, and it is consequently important to examine both the views of officers towards victims and towards victim support in particular. The support of senior police officers has in the past been crucial to the establishment of good links between police forces and local VSSs. Maguire and Corbett (1987) argued that it was Superintendents or Chief Inspectors in charge of stations, or responsible for maintaining contact with victim support, who have been the key figures in this regard. This certainly seemed to be the case in the two forces involved in this study, where close ties were maintained by the (Detective) Chief Inspectors responsible for liaison with the local VSSs.

Both areas in the study had long-standing and well developed VSSs, and the co-ordinators of the schemes maintained close contacts with the liaison officers at the local police stations. In both areas the police automatically referred to the VSS all cases of domestic burglary, all offences against the person (including robbery and murder), all sex offences (including rape), criminal damage and arson at domestic premises. Moreover, in one of the areas any crime, irrespective of type, in which the victim was over 60 years of age, was referred.

Maguire and Corbett (1987) interviewed senior police officers about their attitudes towards victim support and found their views to be particularly important in influencing the types and numbers of cases referred to many schemes. The gap in knowledge, which still exists, is what those officers (usually of lower rank) who come into daily contact with victims think about the services VSSs provide. Key questions include whether, for example, they regard VSSs as beneficial and, indeed, how often they inform victims of the existence of a local scheme.

The breadth of knowledge about local victim support schemes amongst officers in this study varied considerably. Only six of the 50 officers said that they did not know how the local VSS worked: the others had some basic understanding of the procedures involved in referring victims to the local scheme. Most officers knew that [some] crime reports were passed on to the local VSS who then made decisions about which victims to visit. The accuracy and quality of the information that officers possessed appeared to be related to the degree to which they had had personal contact with, or some other experience of, victim support. One VSS had an office adjacent to a police station and consequently officers who had worked in this station tended to be better informed about the work of the scheme than their colleagues. Similarly, those officers who had had cause to contact the VSS directly, or had had some feedback from victims who had been visited by a VSS volunteer also appeared to possess more information about victim support than colleagues who had had little or no contact with the local scheme.

Most officers said that they did not routinely tell victims about the local scheme, nor did they ask them whether they would be interested in a visit. This, they suggested, was generally in accordance with what they had been told about the formal procedures for passing on details of victims via the local liaison officer to the co-ordinator of the VSS. Although it was open to officers, if they wished, to suggest to their liaison officer that certain victims appeared, in their opinion, to be in need of support, most seemed to feel that this was unnecessary because of the formal referral procedure. Approximately two-thirds of the officers interviewed said that it was not their job to inform victims about this service because there was an established procedure in operation in the station which would ensure that those victims who needed support would be referred to the scheme.

Nevertheless, there were two officers who routinely informed all victims about the local VSS, and 11 who said that they informed those victims who they considered to be in particular need of support. Interestingly, these victims, when classified, were distinguished by officers according to certain personal characteristics, attributes or forms of behaviour, rather than by the nature of the offence. They were described as generally being very upset or distressed as a result of their experience. When pressed, officers said that it was the old, the infirm and those living alone who tended to fall into this category.

31

At the other end of the spectrum, there were a small number of officers—about one-tenth of those interviewed—who suggested that victim support was rarely necessary. One officer said that he had never referred anyone to the VSS as he had never encountered a victim who needed it. Officers expressing views such as this were very much in a minority, and generally victim support was viewed in a positive light.

The officers in the study were asked what they thought of the work of the local VSS, and, although there were some who could draw on little practical experience, almost all expressed positive opinions. Several expressed the opinion, that it was important to have VSSs as they were the only counter-balance to the proliferation of organisations that had developed to serve the needs of offenders. The benefits of victim support were generally viewed as being of two types; those accruing to the victim and those to the police. As far as victims were concerned, officers pointed to the importance of both emotional and practical support. Some said that they thought that the VSS probably only offered 'tea and sympathy' but that this was nonetheless important; others referred to more practical or material help that may be offered:

> One of the important things about the victim support scheme is that it has independent, experienced people who will stick a lock on a door, and will reassure old people.

The fact that the service was offered by volunteers was singled out by several officers for special praise. Volunteers were perceived as 'having no axe to grind' and as providing a valuable service without getting in the way of day-to-day police work. One officer referring to the development of the local VSS went as far as to say:

> Best thing that ever happened to this county if you ask me. One volunteer is worth 10 pressed men.

Victim support was also seen as being of direct benefit to the police themselves. When asked about the importance of the work of the scheme in their local area the one thing cited by officers more than anything else was the potential saving of time. Almost all the officers took the view that they did not have sufficient time to deal with victims in the way they would always want. Victim support was seen as providing a service that the police either never or no longer had the time to provide. This was frequently referred to as 'social' or 'welfare policing', in contrast to crime detection. Most officers felt that a proportion of victims wanted more attention than they were able to give, and they interpreted this in a quantitative rather than a qualitative manner. In other words they felt that anything further that they could do for victims would either involve, or would simply consist of, spending more time with them, rather than providing a different type of service. All officers complained of lack of time and consequently any further time that could be given by a victim support volunteer was seen as being beneficial. Victim support was generally perceived by police officers not as being qualitatively different from the 'welfare' side of police work, but as one officer said it was the 'sort of thing we would do if we had the time'.

A different type of benefit for the police was identified by more senior officers. They suggested that victim support was good 'public relations' for the police. Again, this was related to time. Police officers, they argued, do not have sufficient time to take into account all the needs that victims have. Although an officer dealing with a crime can show that 'something is being done', for example, by arranging for the scenes of crime officer to attend, or the crime prevention officer to call, or by putting the victim in touch with the social services, being directly involved in making arrangements for a victim support volunteer to visit shows the police in a caring light. It is another way, they felt, in which the police could, albeit indirectly, 'keep in touch with their constituency'. As Maguire and Corbett (1987) noted, some police officers have suggested 'that the existence of schemes helps remove pressure on the police to do more for victims themselves'. A few officers clearly felt that the existence of victim support enabled them to concentrate on 'real' police work. As one DC said: '. . . it's my job to deal with offenders, not victims'.

Not all the comments received about victim support, however, were positive. No officers were strongly against the idea or practice of victim support, but some did express reservations. The major criticism, and one usually derived from experience, was that there was a proportion of victims who did not like their name being passed on by the police to the VSS without their knowledge or consent. Maguire and Corbett (1987) found that 22 per cent of the victims in their sample reported a negative initial reaction to victim support, although the majority of these were welcoming once volunteers had had a chance to explain why they were calling. A small number of officers in this study reported having been criticised by victims who were annoyed that they had been contacted by the VSS. They argued that these victims did not like the intrusion caused by the unsolicited visit and that, in future, their permission should be sought before passing their name on. Generally, however, most officers reported having had positive responses from victims after they had been visited by a scheme volunteer.

The other major criticism levelled at VSSs was that they were not always staffed by the right type of volunteers. The VSS trainer in one of the forces said that the local scheme needed to have a more representative class and sex ratio, as they tended to attract mainly female and middle-class volunteers. This is a problem that besets many voluntary organisations and it is difficult to see any easy way of overcoming such inconsistencies in recruitment.

Some officers pointed to areas in which they thought that the VSS could do more with regard to victims. The most frequently mentioned area was support for the victim in court. Officers argued that, particularly since the introduction of the Crown Prosecution Service (CPS), they had little opportunity to sort out any problems that the victim/witness might have in court and that, consequently, there was much that victim support volunteers in court might be able to achieve. This point has recently been reinforced by the findings of the NAVSS Working Party on The Victim in Court (NAVSS, 1988).

Others felt that work with bereaved relatives was important. Another suggestion was that there ought to be more direct contact between officers and their local VSS. The view was put forward that although most officers knew of the existence of the local VSS, they would be much more likely to make full use of its services if they had more practical knowledge of its work. This general feeling was confirmed in the research which found that it was those officers who had had direct contact with the local VSS who tended to have the more positive views of victim support. Secondly, these officers also tended to be the ones who cut through the bureaucracy of the referral system and contacted the VSS directly in what they considered to be particularly urgent cases.

Thirty-one of the 100 victims in the sample had been contacted by victim support. Of these victims, three had been told about victim support in advance of being contacted by them. All three had been told by the police. Not all victims had been visited by a victim support volunteer, some being contacted by letter or telephone. A number of victims had been impressed by the speed with which they had been contacted.

When asked how they felt about being contacted by the VSS most victims reported having no strong feelings. However, there were four who were unhappy about the fact that the police had passed on their name and address without asking and/or telling them. They felt that they should have been warned. Despite these reservations all the comments about the work of the schemes were positive:

> . . . they just turned up. I was a bit suspicious at first. But it was OK. They offered to help and seemed very nice.

Generally respondents said that the VSS had offered help, reassurance and someone to contact if needed. Seven victims had been offered specific help with CICS or insurance claims and these victims were particularly appreciative of victim support. Interestingly, when victims were questioned about having been visited by agencies other than the police in connection with the offence, few could remember the term 'victim support [scheme]'. They were able to remember that someone had called on them and offered to help, but rarely could they remember what the organisation was called. The impression given by those victims who had been contacted was that although they were pleased to have been contacted, they did not really feel that they were particularly needy and that, consequently, there was little that the VSS could do. A frequently voiced opinion was that 'I didn't really need any help, but I'm sure there must be lots of people who would'. Even in what appeared to be one of the most serious cases, where an 80 year old man had been bound and gagged whilst his house was searched by intruders, victim support was described as being probably better for those who really need it. He commented:

I think its a good idea, but it's probably only necessary for those who have been really shaken up. It didn't really bother me, so I said thank you but no thank you.

A number of those interviewed were reluctant to regard themselves as a 'victim' and a few were surprised when the label 'victim' was used. Few of those in the sample saw their problems as major or perceived themselves as being in need of specialist help. However, as was suggested above, the two areas of criminal injuries compensation and insurance were the major exceptions to this.

In summary, the majority of those interviewed spoke positively of victim support. Although some of the victims were reluctant to see themselves as 'needy', they were usually of the opinion that there would be others who would both appreciate and be in need of such a service. The majority of police officers saw victim support as being of benefit to both victims and the police. Most officers said that they had too little time available to spend with victims. As a consequence, VSSs were viewed as important by the police precisely because they were seen as being able to do those things that the police would do themselves if they had the time.

6 Conclusions

Home Office circular 20/1988 states that: 'victims cannot realistically expect the police to apprehend every offender, nor that every prosecution will be successful. However, many victims welcome *information* about progress in the enquiries made into the offence against them, and in any resulting prosecution'. Accordingly the circular asks Chief Officers to review their arrangements for keeping victims informed of the progress and outcome of investigations and prosecutions resulting from offences against them, with a view to making these procedures as effective as possible within the constraints of existing resources.

Whilst it might be argued, ideally, that *all* victims should be kept updated about *all* developments in their case, or even regularly informed that there had not been any developments, this is unlikely to be a practical option. Consequently, any recommendations regarding changes in current practices in the provision of case-status information for victims must, as was suggested in the circular, take into account the considerable claims on finite police resources that already exist. This research, therefore, not only considered victims' experiences of their contacts with the police and their needs and priorities for information, but also police officers' experiences of dealing with victims of crime, and the constraints within which they have to do such work.

The major priority within the project was to identify those pieces or areas of information that victims most frequently or most strongly argue are important to their sense of wellbeing and satisfaction. This research suggests that the major problems experienced by victims in relation to information-provision occur in the later rather than the early stages of a case. Overall, 85 per cent of victims were either very satisfied or satisfied with their initial contact with the police, a higher proportion than those reported by Burns-Howell (1982), Burrows (1986), Howley (1982) or Maguire (1982), which may suggest that some improvements have been made since those research projects were conducted.

Satisfaction and dissatisfaction appeared to be related to the manner in which the police were perceived by the victim to be dealing with the case. Concern, sympathy and interest led to feelings of satisfaction; conversely, where these were missing dissatisfaction ensued. The general demeanour and behaviour of the investigating officer appeared to be crucial, and this reinforces the message of Shapland *et al.*'s (1985) research, that it is respect and concern that victims desire. Much of the research that has looked at the relationship between the police and victims of crime has suggested that in many ways the police look upon the victim as a resource, as a source of information and evidence which enables them to succeed in the primary task of policing—that of apprehending and prosecuting offenders. It is becoming increasingly apparent, however, that victims of crime find this relationship unsatisfactory. What they appear to desire is to be treated rather more like *customers* and rather less like an *informational resource*.

Whilst most victims found their initial meetings satisfactory the flow of information between police and victim tended to diminish substantially after an arrest had been made and as the case subsequently passed through the various stages of the criminal justice system. Although in most cases information about arrests was passed on to victims, details of the outcome of the case, particularly details from court, appeared to reach the victim, if at all, in a much more haphazard way. This was the greatest single source of dissatisfaction reported by the victims in the study. Two-thirds of victims said that they thought that the police *should* have let them know the outcome. The single most important piece of information victims wished to have was the knowledge that the case was 'closed'. This might simply mean that there had not been an arrest and that no further inquiries were to be made, that no charges were being made or, for example, that a conviction had been secured. 'Closure' was an extremely important component in the process by which victims came to terms with what had happened to them. Whatever the outcome, victims suggested, it was extremely important for them to be able to feel that the experience was over.

There was general agreement from the police officers in the study that it was important to pass on information about the outcome of the case to victims. Nevertheless, officers and victims had different perceptions of what constituted an 'outcome'. Officers rarely recognised that no arrest or no progress constituted an 'outcome' and they often assumed that victims would not expect or want to hear that nothing had happened. Given the importance of such information to the victim it would appear that the establishment of procedures by which victims are ensured of being informed of the closure of the case, whether that be marked by the discontinuation of enquiries, the decision not to bring charges or the sentence of the court, will be crucial to improved police-victim relations.

The lack of information and the consequent reduction in satisfaction were attributable not only to differing perceptions about 'outcomes' but also to organisational difficulties which made the passage of such information more complicated. As cases progressed, officers argued that they tended to have less information about them, a difficulty said to have been complicated by the introduction of the CPS, which had lessened the likelihood of officers attending court. The results of court proceedings could take up to two months to be fed back to the police. By this time, they felt it was too late to be of use, either because they assumed that the victim would have got the information from another source or simply because after such a period of time the officers were likely to be involved in other work and were consequently unable to keep track of all the cases they had previously been involved in. Potential solutions to this problem are likely to be complicated by the fact that several agencies are involved. Smoothing the flow of this information will necessitate liaison between the police, CPS and the courts. However, even if a method of passing the results back quickly to the police is negotiated, it would still seem to be impractical to expect the original investigating officers to feed this information to the victim. Therefore, making sure such information is regularly passed on is likely to require a central point where the information is collected, stored and then—by whichever means is decided upon but, possibly, case-status officers—passed on to the victim.

Because of the difficulties many police forces faced in meeting victims' informational needs the onus for obtaining such information was often placed on the victim. However, few victims made enquiries themselves. Many victims felt unable or *were* unable to make enquiries at the police station. Inhibiting factors included lack of knowledge as to whom to contact, but others were of the opinion that they should not initiate contact with the police—a feeling few, if any, could explain.

What is important here is that despite the fact that all the officers in the study said that they gave victims a telephone number where they could be reached, not all the victims remembered having received this, and of those that did some made unsuccessful attempts at contact and others felt unable even to try. Of those victims who did make enquiries many reported a general lack of success. They frequently found that the officer they wished to contact was unavailable because of holidays, shifts, etc, and that there was rarely someone else readily available who could provide the information they required. Consequently, any attempts at improving information-flow between police and victims will need to consider the procedures by which victims attempt to gain information about their cases. Given that the police cannot be expected to make contact with victims every time new information arises, making it easier for victims to contact *someone*—not necessarily the investigating officer—who will be able to give them some information about progress in their case, may well lead to a considerable advance on current practice.

Concern that information about services for victims—such as criminal injuries and court-ordered compensation—should be consistently conveyed to victims has recently found expression in Home Office circulars 20/1988 and 85/1988 as well as a related leaflet that has been produced for distribution to victims of crime. The results of this study suggest that not all victims are provided with reliable information about compensation and that whilst this is, in part, due to similar organisational difficulties that hamper the passage of case-status information, similarly, many police officers simply do not appear to possess sufficient reliable information about these services.

39

Lack of reliable information was not the sole cause of failing to inform victims adequately. In relation to the CICS, for example, some officers felt that it was simply not their responsibility but rather that of another agency. Moreover, officers who did pass on information about the CICS to victims did not do so in all cases. Instead they appeared to distinguish between 'deserving' victims and those they felt were 'undeserving'. Distinctions were also made between cases involving 'serious' and 'minor' injuries. In general, the police officers in the study appeared to lack basic information about the operation of the CICS and of court-ordered compensation.

Compensation as a general issue—whether it be from the offender or the state—appeared to cause a fair amount of confusion among officers. They were both unsure about the exact procedures involved with each and what their role was meant to be. Some officers, for example, assumed that the existence of the CICS meant that the courts merely dealt with compensation for loss or damage. The end result was that a considerable proportion of victims did not receive information and advice about what was available to them and, in some cases, undoubtedly missed out on compensation. Although consideration may well have to be given to the whole area of information-provision for victims, the area of compensation is clearly one where more systematic training, advice and information for police officers would be likely to be of benefit to victims.

How, then, is the whole question of information for victims to be approached? The first, and perhaps major, question considered in this study was what information do victims say they most need, and yet frequently miss out on? Generally speaking, these were found to relate to what was the 'end' of the case for the victim. It appears from this study that police forces, if they are going to reconsider their information-provision procedures, would do well to concentrate—in conjunction with other agencies such as the CPS and the courts—on the following points in the development of cases: when enquiries cease even though no arrest has been made—(clearly, 'crime screening' may make this a particularly crucial informational stage for victims); when an arrest is made and charges brought; when charges are dropped; and on the occasion of court appearances, the setting of bail and the result of the court hearing. In practical terms it ought not to be too difficult to ensure that *all* victims, and not merely witnesses, are informed of impending court dates and that, similarly, information about court results is routinely passed on by the courts not only to the police but also to victims.

Clearly the establishment of a set of procedures that would ensure, where appropriate, that all victims received all the information listed above would be likely to be extremely resource intensive and probably organisationally problematic. It might also be considered to be an inefficient use of resources, as some victims would simply not be interested in receiving such information. As a consequence it might be more practical to give thought not only to setting in place standardised automatic information-provision procedures but also to improving the methods by which general case-status information is collected and stored in police stations and provided for victims when requested. If such information was easily accessible to specifically designated staff (possibly a case-status officer)—and this would require the co-operation of other agencies such as the courts and the CPS—some emphasis might be placed on victims' responsibility for making inquiries about progress in their case. This would clearly require some 'education' of victims. It would be necessary, for example, to ensure that victims were routinely made aware that they could make such enquiries and that they were given the requisite telephone numbers and the names of the appropriate members of staff to approach.

A reliable system by which victims could be reasonably assured of up-to-date information about some aspects of their case would obviate the necessity for a comprehensive set of information-provision procedures under which the responsibility for keeping victims informed fell entirely upon the police in conjunction with the courts, the CPS and possibly victims support schemes. This would, of course, not remove the burden entirely from the police, for there would continue to be a need for victims to be informed of certain developments such as the discontinuation of enquiries, court dates and results, but it would ensure that for the rest of the time resources and effort were not being expended needlessly passing on unwanted information. It appears in conclusion, then, that the establishment of a system in which there is a balance between automatic provision and demand-led supply of information will be the most effective method of improving on the current situation without over-stretching existing resources.

References

Burns-Howell, A. J. *et al.* (1982). *Policing Strategy: Organisational or Victim Needs?* Unpublished report. Police College, Bramshill.

Burrows, J. (1986). *Burglary: Police Actions and Victim's Views.* Research and Planning Unit Paper 37. Home Office: London.

Chambers, G. and Millar, A. (1983). *Investigating Sexual Assault.* Edinburgh: HMSO.

Ekblom, P. and Heal, K. (1982). *The Police Response to Calls From the Public.* Home Office research and Planning Unit Paper 9. London: Home Office.

Hough, J. M. and Mayhew, P. (1983). *The British Crime Survey: First Report.* Home Office Research Study No. 76. London: HMSO.

Howley, J. A. (1982). *Victim—Police Interaction and its Effects on Public Attitudes to the Police.* Unpublished MSc Thesis. Cranfield Institute of Technology.

Jones, S. J. (1983). 'Community Policing in Devon and Cornwall: Some Research Findings on the Relationship between the Public and the Police'. In Bennet, T. (ed). *The Future of Policing.* Cropwood Conferences Series No. 15. Cambridge: Institute of Criminology.

Maguire, M. (1982). *Burglary in a Dwelling: the offence, the offender and the victim.* London: Heinemann Educational Books.

Maguire, M. (1984). 'Meeting the needs of burglary victims: questions for the police and the criminal justice system'. In Clarke, R. V. G. and Hope, T. *Coping with Burglary: Research Perspectives on Policy.* Boston: Kluwer Nijhoff.

Maguire, M. and Corbett, C. (1987). *The Effects of Crime and the Work of Victims Support Schemes.* Aldershot: Gower.

Mawby, R. (1979). *Policing the City.* Saxon House.

Miers, D. (1978). *Responses to Victimisation.* Abingdon: Professional Books.

Miers, D. (1980). 'Victim Compensation as a Labelling Process'. *Victimology,* Vol. 5, pp. 3–16.

National Association of Victims Support Schemes (1988). 'The Victim In Court: Report of a Working Party'. London: NAVSS.

Newburn, T. (1988). *The Use and Enforcement of Compensation Orders in Magistrates' Courts*. Home Office Research Study No. 102. London: HMSO.

Shapland, J. and Cohen, D. (1987). 'Facilities for Victims: The Role of the Police and the Courts'. *Criminal Law Review*, January, pp. 28–38.

Shapland, J., Willmore, J. and Duff, P. (1985). *Victims in the Criminal Justice System*. Aldershot: Gower.

Smith, D. J. and Gray, J. (1985). *Police and People in London*. Aldershot: Gower.

Southgate, P. and Ekblom, P. (1984). *Contacts between Police and Public*. Home Office Research Study No. 77. London: HMSO.

Sparks, R., Genn, H. and Dodd, D. (1977). *Surveying Victims*. London: John Wiley.

Publications

Titles already published for the Home Office

Studies in the Causes of Delinquency and the Treatment of Offenders (SCDTO)

1. Prediction methods in relation to borstal training. Hermann Mannheim and Leslie T. Wilkins. 1955. viii+276pp. (11 340051 9).
2. *Time spent awaiting trial. Evelyn Gibson. 1960. v+45pp. (34–368–2).
3. *Delinquent generations. Leslie T. Wilkins. 1960. iv+20pp.
4. *Murder. Evelyn Gibson and S. Klein. 1961. iv+44pp. (11 340054 3).
5. Persistent criminals. A study of all offenders liable to preventive detention in 1956. W. H. Hammond and Edna Chayen. 1963. ix+237pp. (34–368–5).
6. *Some statistical and other numerical techniques for classifying individuals. P. McNaughton-Smith. 1965. v+33pp. (34–368–6).
7. Probation research: a preliminary report. Part I. General outline of research. Part II. Study of Middlesex probation area (SOMPA). Steven Folkard, Kate Lyon, Margaret M. Carver and Erica O'Leary. 1966. vi+58pp. (11 340374 7).
8. *Probation research: national study of probation. Trends and regional comparisons in probation (England and Wales). Hugh Barr and Erica O'Leary. 1966. vii+51pp. (34–368–8).
9. *Probation research. A survey of group work in the probation service. Hugh Barr. 1966. vii+94pp. (34–368–9).
10. *Types of delinquency and home background. A validation study of Hewitt and Jenkins' hypothesis. Elizabeth Field. 1967. vi+21pp. (34–368–10).
11. *Studies of female offenders. No. 1—Girls of 16–20 years sentenced to borstal or detention centre training in 1963. No. 2—Women offenders in the Metropolitan Police District in March and April 1957. No. 3—A description of women in prison on January 1, 1965. Nancy Goodman and Jean Price. 1967. v+78pp. (34–368–11).
12. *The use of the Jesness Inventory on a sample of British probationers. Martin Davies. 1967. iv+20pp. (34–368–12).
13. *The Jesness Inventory: application to approved school boys. Joy Mott. 1969. iv+27pp. (11 340063 2).

Home Office Research Studies (HORS)

1. *Workloads in children's departments. Eleanor Grey. 1969. vi+75pp. (11 340101 9).
2. *Probationers in their social environment. A study of male probationers aged 17–20, together with an analysis of those reconvicted within twelve months. Martin Davies. 1969. vii+204pp. (11 340102 7).
3. *Murder 1957 to 1968. A Home Office Statistical Division report on murder in England and Wales. Evelyn Gibson and S. Klein (with annex by the Scottish Home and Health Department on murder in Scotland). 1969. vi+94pp. (11 340103 5).
4. Firearms in crime. A Home Office Statistical Division report on indictable offences involving firearms in England and Wales. A. D. Weatherhead and B. M. Robinson. 1970. viii+39pp. (11 340104 3).

* Out of print.

45

5. *Financial penalties and probation. Martin Davies. 1970. vii+39pp. (11 340105 1).

6. *Hostels for probationers. A study of the aims, working and variations in effectiveness of male probation hostels with special reference to the influence of the environment on delinquency. Ian Sinclair. 1971. ix+200pp. (11 340106 X).

7. *Prediction methods in criminology—including a prediction study of young men on probation. Frances H. Simon. 1971. xi+234pp. (11 340107 8).

8. *Study of the juvenile liaison scheme in West Ham 1961–65. Marilyn Taylor. 1971. vi+46pp. (11 340108 6).

9. *Explorations in after-care. I—After-care units in London, Liverpool and Manchester. Martin Silberman (Royal London Prisoners' Aid Society) and Brenda Chapman. II—After-care hostels receiving a Home Office grant. Ian Sinclair and David Snow (HORU). III—St. Martin of Tours House, Aryeh Leissner (National Bureau for Co-operation in Child Care). 1971. xi+140pp. (11 340109 4).

10. A survey of adoption in Great Britain. Eleanor Grey in collaboration with Ronald M. Blunden. 1971. ix+168pp. (11 340110 8).

11. *Thirteen-year-old approved school boys in 1962s. Elizabeth Field, W. H. Hammond and J. Tizard. 1971. ix+46pp. (11 340111 6).

12. Absconding from approved schools. R. V. G. Clarke and D. N. Martin. 1971. vi+146pp. (11 340112 4).

13. An experiment in personality assessment of young men remanded in custody. H. Sylvia Anthony. 1972. viii+79pp. (11 340113 2).

14. *Girl offenders aged 17–20 years. I—Statistics relating to girl offenders aged 17–20 years from 1960 to 1970. II—Re-offending by girls released from borstal or detention centre training. III—The problems of girls released from borstal training during their period on after-care. Jean Davies and Nancy Goodman. 1972. v+77pp. (11 340114 0).

15. *The controlled trial in institutional research—paradigm or pitfall for penal evaluators? R. V. G. Clarke and D. B. Cornish. 1972. v+33pp. (11 340115 9).

16. *A survey of fine enforcement. Paul Softley. 1973. v+65pp. (11 340116 7).

17. *An index of social environment—designed for use in social work menum research. Martin Davies. 1973. vi+63pp. (11 340117 5).

18. *Social enquiry reports and the probation service. Martin Davies and Andrea Knopf. 1973. v+49pp. (11 340118 3).

19. *Depression, psychopathic personality and attempted suicide in a borstal sample. H. Sylvia Anthony. 1973. viii+44p. (0 11 340119 1).

20. *The use of bail and custody by London magistrates' courts before and after the Criminal Justice Act 1967. Frances Simon and Mollie Weatheritt. 1974. vi+78pp. (0 11 340120 5).

21. *Social work in the environment. A study of one aspect of probation practice. Martin Davies, with Margaret Rayfield, Alaster Calder and Tony Fowles. 1974. ix+151pp. (0 11 340121 3).

22. Social work in prison. An experiment in the use of extended contact with offenders. Margaret Shaw. 1974. viii+154pp. (0 11 340122 1).

23. Delinquency amongst opiate users. Joy Mott and Marilyn Taylor. 1974. vi+31pp. (0 11 340663 0).

24. IMPACT. Intensive matched probation and after-care treatment. Vol. I—The design of the probation experiment and an interim evaluation. M. S. Folkard, A. J. Fowles, B. C. McWilliams, W. McWilliams, D. D. Smith, D. E. Smith and G. R. Walmsley. 1974. v+54pp. (0 11 340664 9).

25. The approved school experience. An account of boys' experiences of training under differing regimes of approved schools, with an attempt to evaluate the effectiveness of that training. Anne B. Dunlop. 1974. vii+124pp. .(0 11 340665 7).

26. *Absconding from open prisons. Charlotte Banks, Patricia Mayhew and R. J. Sapsford. 1975. viii+89pp. (0 11 340666 5).

27. Driving while disqualified. Sue Kriefman. 1975. vi+136pp. (0 11 340667 3).

---

* Out of print.

28. Some male offenders' problems. I—Homeless offenders in Liverpool. W. McWilliams. II—Casework with short-term prisoners. Julie Holborn. 1975. x+147pp. (0 11 340668 1).

29. *Community service orders. K. Pease, P. Durkin, I. Earnshaw, D. Payne and J. Thorpe. 1975. viii+80pp. (0 11 340669 X).

30. Field Wing Bail Hostel: the first nine months. Frances Simon and Sheena Wilson. 1975. viii+55pp. (0 11 340670 3).

31. Homicide in England and Wales 1967–1971. Evelyn Gibson. 1975. iv+59pp. (0 11 340753 X).

32. Residential treatment and its effects on delinquency. D. B. Cornish and R. V. G. Clarke. 1975. vi+74pp. (0 11 340672 X).

33. Further studies of female offenders. Part A: Borstal girls eight years after release. Nancy Goodman, Elizabeth Maloney and Jean Davies. Part B: The sentencing of women at the London Higher Courts. Nancy Goodman, Paul Durkin and Janet Halton. Part C: Girls appearing before a juvenile court. Jean Davies. 1976. vi+114pp. (0 11 340673 8).

34. *Crime as opportunity. P. Mayhew, R. V. G. Clarke, A. Sturman and J. M. Hough. 1976. vii+36pp. (0 11 340674 6).

35. The effectiveness of sentencing: a review of the literature. S. R. Brody. 1976. v+89pp. (0 11 340675 4).

36. IMPACT. Intensive matched probation and after-care treatment. Vol. II—The results of the experiment. M. S. Folkard, D. E. Smith and D. D. Smith 1976. xi+40pp. (0 11 340676 2).

37. Police cautioning in England and Wales. J. A. Ditchfield. 1976. v+31pp. (0 11 340677 0).

38. Parole in England and Wales. C. P. Nuttall, with E. E. Barnard, A. J. Fowles, A. Frost, W. H. Hammond, P. Mayhew, K. Pease, R. Tarling and M. J. Weatheritt. 1977. vi+90pp. (0 11 340678 9).

39. Community service assessed in 1976. K. Pease, S. Billingham and I. Earnshaw. 1977. vi+29pp. (0 11 340679 7).

40. Screen violence and film censorship: a review of research. Stephen Brody. 1977. vii+179pp. (0 11 340680 0).

41. *Absconding from borstals. Gloria K. Laycock. 1977. v+82pp. (0 11 340681 9).

42. Gambling: a review of the literature and its implications for policy and research. D. B. Cornish. 1978. xii+284pp. (0 11 340682 7).

43. Compensation orders in magistrates' courts. Paul Softley. 1978. v+41pp. (0 11 340683 5).

44. Research in criminal justice. John Croft. 1978. iv+16pp. (0 11 340684 3).

45. Prison welfare: an account of an experiment at Liverpool. A. J. Fowles. 1978. v+34pp. (0 11 340685 1).

46. Fines in magistrates' courts. Paul Softley. 1978. v+42pp. (0 11 340686 X).

47. Tackling vandalism. R. V. G. Clarke (editor), F. J. Gladstone, A. Sturman and Sheena Wilson (contributors). 1978. vi+91pp. (0 11 340687 8).

48. Social inquiry reports: a survey. Jennifer Thorpe. 1979. vi+55pp. (0 11 340688 6).

49. Crime in public view. P. Mayhew, R. V. G. Clarke, J. N. Burrows, J. M. Hough and S. W. C. Winchester. 1979. v+36pp. (0 11 340689 4).

50. *Crime and the community. John Croft. 1979. v+16pp. (0 11 340690 8).

51. Life-sentence prisoners. David Smith (editor), Christopher Brown, Joan Worth, Roger Sapsford and Charlotte Banks (contributors). 1979. iv+51pp. (0 11 340691 6).

52. Hostels for offenders. Jane E. Andrews, with an appendix by Bill Sheppard. 1979. v+30pp. (0 11 340692 4).

53. Previous convictions, sentence and reconviction: a statistical study of a sample of 5,000 offenders convicted in January 1971. G. J. O. Phillpotts and L. B. Lancucki. 1979. v+55pp. (0 11 340693 2).

54. Sexual offences, consent and sentencing. Roy Walmsley and Karen White. 1979. vi+77pp. (0 11 340694 0).

---

* Out of print.

55. Crime prevention and the police. John Burrows, Paul Ekblom and Kevin Heal. 1979. v+37pp. (0 11 340695 9).

56. Sentencing practice in magistrates' courts. Roger Tarling, with the assistance of Mollie Weatheritt. 1979. vii+54pp. (0 11 340696 7).

57. Crime and comparative research. John Croft. 1979. iv+16pp. (0 11 340697 5).

58. Race , crime and arrests. Philip Stevens and Carole F. Willis. 1979. v+69pp. (0 11 340698 3).

59. Research and criminal policy. John Croft. 1980. iv+14pp. (0 11 340699 1).

60. Junior attendance centres. Anne B. Dunlop. 1980. v+47pp. (0 11 340700 9).

61. Police interrogation: an observational study in four police stations. Paul Softley, with the assistance of David Brown, Bob Forde, George Mair and David Moxon. 1980. vii+67pp. (0 11 340701 7).

62. Co-ordinating crime prevention efforts. F. J. Gladstone. 1980. v+74pp. (0 11 340702 5).

63. Crime prevention publicity: an assessment. D. Riley and P. Mayhew. 1980. v+47pp. (0 11 340703 3).

64. Taking offenders out of circulation. Stephen Brody and Roger Tarling. 1980. v+46pp. (0 11 340704 1).

65. *Alcoholism and social policy: are we on the right lines? Mary Tuck. 1980. v+30pp. (0 11 340705 X).

66. Persistent petty offenders. Suzan Fairhead. 1981. vi+78pp. (0 11 340706 8).

67. Crime control and the police. Pauline Morris and Kevin Heal. 1981. v+71pp. (0 11 340707 6).

68. Ethnic minorities in Britain: a study of trends in their position since 1961. Simon Field, George Mair, Tom Rees and Philip Stevens. 1981. v+48pp. (0 11 340708 4).

69. Managing criminological research. John Croft. 1981. iv+17pp. (0 11 340709 2).

70. Ethnic minorities, crime and policing: a survey of the experiences of West Indians and whites. Mary Tuck and Peter Southgate. 1981. iv+54pp. (0 11 340765 3).

71. Contested trials in magistrates' courts. Julie Vennard. 1982. v+32pp. (0 11 340766 1).

72. Public disorder: a review of research and a study in one inner city area. Simon Field and Peter Southgate. 1982. v+77pp. (0 11 340767 X).

73. Clearing up crime. John Burrows and Roger Tarling. 1982. vii+31pp. (0 11 340768 8).

74. Residential burglary: the limits of prevention. Stuart Winchester and Hilary Jackson. 1982. v+47pp. (0 11 340769 6).

75. Concerning crime. John Croft. 1982. v+16pp. (0 11 340770 X).

76. The British Crime Survey: first report. Mike Hough and Pat Mayhew. 1983. v+62pp. (0 11 340786 6).

77. Contacts between police and public: findings from the British Crime Survey. Peter Southgate and Paul Ekblom. 1984. v+42pp. (0 11 340771 8).

78. Fear of crime in England and Wales. Michael Maxfield. 1984. v+57pp. (0 11 340772 6).

79. Crime and police effectiveness. Ronald V. Clarke and Mike Hough. 1984. iv+33pp. (0 11 340773 3).

80. The attitudes of ethnic minorities. Simon Field. 1984. v+49pp. (0 11 340774 2).

81. Victims of crime: the dimensions of risk. Michael Gottfredson. 1984. v+54pp. (0 11 340775 0).

82. The tape recording of police interviews with suspects: an interim report. Carole Willis. 1984. v+45pp. (0 11 340776 9).

83. Parental supervision and juvenile delinquency. David Riley and Margaret Shaw. 1985. v+90pp. (0 11 340799 8).

84. Adult prisons and prisoners in England and Wales 1970-1982: a review of the findings of social research. Joy Mott. 1985. vi+73pp. (0 11 340801 3).

85. Taking account of crime: key findings from the 1984 British Crime Survey. Mike Hough and Pat Mayhew. 1985. vi+115pp. (0 11 341810 2).

86. Implementing crime prevention measures. Tim Hope. 1985. vi+82pp. (0 11 340812 9).

---

* Out of print.

87. Resettling refugees: the lessons of research. Simon Field. 1985. vi+66pp. (0 11 340815 3).

88. Investigating burglary: the measurement of police performance. John Burrows. 1986. vi+36pp. (0 11 340824 2).

89. Personal violence. Roy Walmsley. 1986. vi+87pp. (0 11 340827 7).

90. Police-public encounters. Peter Southgate. 1986. vi+150pp. (0 11 340834 X).

91. Grievance procedures in prisons. John Ditchfield and Claire Austin. 1986. vi+87pp. (0 11 340839 0).

92. The effectiveness of the Forensic Science Service. Malcolm Ramsay. 1987. v+100pp. (0 11 340842 0).

93. The police complaints procedure: a survey of complainant's views. David Brown. 1987. v+98pp. (0 11 340853 6).

94. The validity of the reconviction prediction score. Denis Ward. 1987. vi+46. (0 11 340882 X).

95. Economic aspects of the illicit drug market enforcement policies in the United Kingdom. Adam Wagstaff and Alan Maynard. 1988. vii+156pp. (0 11 340883 8).

96. Schools, disruptive behaviour and delinquency: a review of literature. John Graham. 1988. v+70pp. (0 11 340887 0).

97. The tape recording of police interviews with suspects: a second interim report. Carole Willis, John Macleod and Peter Naish. 1988. vii+97pp. (0 11 340890 0).

98. Triable-either-way cases: Crown court or magistrate's court. David Riley and Julie Vennard. 1988. v+52pp. (0 11 340891 9).

99. Directing patrol work: a study of uniformed policing. John Burrows and Helen Lewis. 1988. v+66pp. (0 11 340891 9).

100. Probation day centres. George Mair. 1988. v+44pp. (0 11 340894 3).

101. Amusement machines: dependency and delinquency. John Graham. 1988. v+48pp. (0 11 340895 1).

102. The use and enforcement of compensation orders in magistrates' courts. Tim Newburn. 1988. v+49pp. (0 11 340896 X).

103. Sentencing practice in the Crown Court. David Moxon. 1988. v+90pp. (0 11 340902 8).

104. Detention at the police station under the Police and Criminal Evidence Act 1984. David Brown. 1988. v+88pp. (0 11 340908 7).

105. Changes in rape offences and sentencing. Charles Lloyd and Roy Walmsley. 1989. vi+53pp. (0 11 340910 9).

106. Concerns about rape. Lorna Smith. 1989. v+48pp. (0 11 340911 7).

107. Domestic violence. Lorna Smith. 1989. v+132pp. (0 11 340925 7).

108. Drinking and disorder: a study of non-metropolitan violence. Mary Tuck. 1989. v+111pp. (0 11 340926 5).

109. Special Security Units. Roy Walmsley. 1989. v+114pp. (0 11 340961 3).

110. Pre-trial delay: the implication of time limits. Patricia Morgan and Julie Vennard. 1989. v+66pp. (0 11 340964 8).

111. The 1988 British Crime Survey. Pat Mayhew, David Elliott and Lizanne Dowds. 1989. v+133pp. (0 11 340965 6).

112. The settlement of claims at the Criminal Injuries Compensation Board. Tim Newburn. 1989. v+41pp. (0 11 340967 2).

113. Race, community groups and service delivery. Simon Field and Hilary Jackson. 1989. v+61pp. (0 11 340972 9).

114. Money Payment Supervision Orders: probation policy and practice. George Mair and Charles Lloyd. 1989. v+40pp. (0 11 340971 0)

115. Suicide and self injury in prison: a literature review. Charles Lloyd. 1989. v+69pp. (0 11 340975 3).

ALSO

Designing out crime. R. V. G Clarke and P. Mayhew (editors). 1980. viii+186pp. (0 11 340732 7).

(This book collects, with an introduction, studies that were originally published in HORS 34, 47, 49, 55, 62 and 63 and which are illustrative of the 'situational' approach to crime prevention.)

Policing today. Kevin Heal, Roger Tarling and John Burrows (editors). v+181pp. (0 11 340800 5).

(This book brings together twelve separate studies on police matters produced during the last few years by the Unit. The collection records some relatively little known contributions to the debate on policing.)

Managing Criminal Justice: a collection of papers. David Moxon (ed.). 1985. vi+222pp. (0 11 340811 0).

(This book brings together a number of studies bearing on the management of the criminal justice system. It includes papers by social scientists and operational researchers working within the Research and Planning Unit, and academic researchers who have studied particular aspects of the criminal process.)

Situational Crime Prevention: from theory into practice. Kevin Heal and Gloria Laycock (editors). 1986. vii+166pp. (0 11 340826 9).

(Following the publication of Designing Out Crime, further research has been completed on the theoretical background to crime prevention. In drawing this work together this book sets down some of the theoretical concerns and discusses the emerging practical issues. It includes contributions by Unit staff as well as academics from this country and abroad.)

Communities and crime reduction. Tim Hope and Margaret Shaw (eds.). 1988. vii+311pp. (0 11 340892 7).

(The central theme of this book is the possibility of preventing crime by building upon the resources of local communities and of active citizens. The specially commissioned chapters, by distinguished international authors, review contemporary research and policy on community crime prevention.)

New directions in police training. Peter Southgate (ed.). 1988. xi+256pp. (0 11 340889 7).

(Training is central to the development of the police role, and particular thought and effort now go into making it more responsive current needs—in order to produce police officers who are both effective and sensitive in their dealing with the public. This book illustrates some of the thinking and research behind these developments.)

The above HMSO publications can be purchased from Government Bookshops or through booksellers.

The following Home Office research publications are available on request from the Home Office Research and Planning Unit, 50 Queen Anne's Gate, London SW1H 9AT.

Research Unit Papers (RUP)

1. Uniformed police work and management technology. J. M. Hough. 1980.
2. Supplementary information on sexual offences and sentencing. Roy Walmsley and Karen White. 1980.
3. Board of visitor adjudications. David Smith, Claire Austin and John Ditchfield. 1981.
4. Day centres and probation. Suzan Fairhead, with the assistance of J. Wilkinson-Grey. 1981.

Research and Planning Unit Papers (RPUP)

5. Ethnic minorities and complaints against the police. Philip Stevens and Carole Willis. 1982.
6. * Crime and public housing. Mike Hough and Pat Mayhew (editors). 1982.
7. * Abstracts of race relations research. George Mair and Philip Stevens (editors). 1982.
8. Police probationer training in race relations. Peter Southgate. 1982.
9. * The police response to calls from the public. Paul Ekblom and Kevin Heal. 1982.
10. City centre crime: a situational approach to prevention. Malcolm Ramsay. 1982.

* Out of print.

11. Burglary in schools: the prospects for prevention. Tim Hope. 1982.

12. * Fine enforcement. Paul Softley and David Moxon. 1982.

13. Vietnamese refugees. Peter Jones. 1982.

14. Community resources for victims of crime. Karen Williams. 1983.

15. The use, effectiveness and impact of police stop and search powers. Carole Willis. 1983.

16. Acquittal rates. Sid Butler. 1983.

17. Criminal justice comparisons: the case of Scotland and England and Wales. Lorna J. F. Smith. 1983.

18. Time taken to deal with juveniles under criminal proceedings. Catherine Frankenburg and Roger Tarling. 1983.

19. Civilian review of complaints against the police: a survey of the United States literature. David C. Brown. 1983.

20. Police action on motoring offences. David Riley. 1983.

21. * Diverting drunks from the criminal justice system. Sue Kingsley and George Mair. 1983.

22. The staff resource implications of an independent prosecution system. Peter R. Jones. 1983.

23. Reducing the prison population: an exploratory study in Hampshire. David Smith, Bill Sheppard, George Mair and Karen Williams. 1984.

24. Criminal justice system model: magistrates' courts sub-model. Susan Rice. 1984.

25. Measures of police effectiveness and efficiency. Ian Sinclair and Clive Miller. 1984.

26. Punishment practice by prison Boards of Visitors. Susan Iles, Adrienne Connors, Chris May and Joy Mott. 1984.

27. * Reparation, conciliation and mediation: current projects and plans in England and Wales. Tony Marshall. 1984.

28. Magistrates' domestic courts: new perspectives. Tony Marshall (editor). 1984.

29. Racism awareness training for the police. Peter Southgate. 1984.

30. Community constables: a study of a policing initiative. David Brown and Susan Iles. 1985.

31. Recruiting volunteers. Hilary Jackson. 1985.

32. Juvenile sentencing: is there a tariff? David Moxon, Peter Jones and Roger Tarling. 1985.

33. Bringing people together: mediation and reparation projects in Great Britain. Tony Marshall and Martin Walpole. 1985.

34. Remands in the absence of the accused. Chris May. 1985.

35. Modelling the criminal justice system. Patricia M. Morgan. 1985.

36. The criminal justice system model: the flow model. Hugh Pullinger. 1986.

37. Burglary: police actions and victim views. John Burrows. 1986.

38. Unlocking community resources: four experimental government small grants schemes. Hilary Jackson. 1986.

39. The cost of discriminating: a review of the literature. Shirley Dex. 1986.

40. Waiting for Crown Court trial: the remand population. Rachel Pearce. 1987.

41. Children's evidence the need for corroboration. Carol Hedderman. 1987.

42. A preliminary study of victim offender mediation and reparation schemes in England and Wales. Gwynn Davis, Jacky Boucherat, David Watson and Adrain Thatcher (Consultant). 1987.

43. Explaining fear of crime: evidence from the 1984 British Crime Survey. Michael Maxfield. 1987.

44. Judgements of crime seriousness: evidence from the 1984 British Crime Survey. Ken Pease. 1988.

45. Waiting time on the day in magistrates' courts: a review of case listings practises. David Moxon and Roger Tarling (editors). 1988.

46. Bail and probation work: the ILPS temporary bail action project. George Mair. 1988.

---

* Out of print.

Research Bulletin

The Research Bulletin is published twice a year and consists mainly of short articles relating to projects which are part of the Home Office Research and Planning Unit's research programme.

Printed in the United Kingdom for HMSO
Dd 292615 C14 2/90 (274867)